Social Media Marketing

Using Facebook, Twitter, Youtube, Instagram And Tumblr To Grow Your Business, Be Successful And Boost Your Sales

Jason Roberts

Copyright 2019 by Jason Roberts - All rights reserved.

This document is geared towards providing exact and reliable information in regards to the topic and issue covered. The publication is sold with the idea that the publisher is not required to render accounting, officially permitted, or otherwise, qualified services. If advice is necessary, legal or professional, a practiced individual in the profession should be ordered.

- From a Declaration of Principles which was accepted and approved equally by a Committee of the American Bar Association and a Committee of Publishers and Associations.

In no way is it legal to reproduce, duplicate, or transmit any part of this document in either electronic means or in printed format. Recording of this publication is strictly prohibited and any storage of this document is not allowed unless with written permission from the publisher. All rights reserved.

The information provided herein is stated to be truthful and consistent, in that any liability, in terms of inattention or otherwise, by any usage or abuse of any policies, processes, or directions contained within is the solitary and utter responsibility of the recipient reader. Under no circumstances will any legal responsibility or blame be held against the publisher for any reparation, damages, or monetary loss due to the information herein, either directly or indirectly.

Respective authors own all copyrights not held by the publisher.

The information herein is offered for informational purposes solely, and is universal as so. The presentation of the information is without contract or any type of guarantee assurance.

The trademarks that are used are without any consent, and the publication of the trademark is without permission or backing by the trademark owner. All trademarks and brands within this book are for clarifying purposes only and are the owned by the owners themselves, not affiliated with this document.

Introduction

I'm happy you decided to invest in *"Social Media Marketing: Using Facebook, Instagram, YouTube To Grow a Business"*.

If you want to expand your business, using the most efficient ways available, then you're in the right place.

This book contains proven steps and strategies on how to grow your business using social networking sites such as Facebook, Instagram, YouTube, Twitter, and Tumblr.

With the rise of technological advances and telecommunication, social interaction in the cyber world has hyped up as well. For business owners who plan to grow their businesses in a fast and assured manner, utilizing these social networking sites is a SURE win. Imagine the scope the worldwide web has.

In the olden times, advertising a product or service was very limited. Depending on the media you use, the scope and coverage was obviously limited. Now, in a span of an hour, your post can go viral and get million views. See the power of social media in today's marketing? Getting to know the features of these platforms will help you ease your tactics in to win your business customers.

Thanks again for downloading this book, I hope you enjoy it!

Table of contents:

1 - The World of Social Media Marketing............ 8

2 - Using Facebook in Social Media Marketing.. 11

3 - Using Instagram in Social Media Marketing. 15

4 - Using YouTube for Social Media Marketing . 19

5 - Using Twitter for Social Media Marketing.... 22

6 - Using Tumblr for Social Media Networking . 26

7 – Advanced Social Media Marketing Tips...... 31

8 – How You Can Build An Effective Social Media Marketing Strategy 35

Conclusion 44

1 - The World of Social Media Marketing

You have got to be living under a rock if you have never ever heard of the rise of technology and social media. Social media refers to websites and applications that promote a social interaction among its users with what they have shared in their accounts or pages. Some of these social media platforms may seem to ring a bell and perhaps, you also have accounts in at least one of these — Facebook, Twitter, Instagram, Google Plus, Tumblr, Pinterest, LinkedIn, YouTube, and many more.

Side-tracking from the usual use of these social media sites and applications, they can also be used as tools for advertising and marketing businesses, both large and small. Using these tools to gain traffic and attention regarding your business is called Social Media Marketing or SMM. In a survey conducted by Hubspot, 92% of the businesses in 2014 have acknowledged the importance of social media in their growth.

This huge population of the marketers in social media is a reflection of the benefits that social media marketing brings. Advertising and marketing using the interactive sites and applications may well create a buzz of your product or service. Since these are social media that promote high conversation and interaction rates of users, the feedback for your business may come immediately. Moreover, when your business gets viral, it gains recognition from the people.

You may put it this way, in social media, you may have a hundred followers or friends that when you post your items or services on your page or account, they will see them. Now, of course, you will not always get to convince these people to buy whatever it is that you are selling but these followers and friends are still your potential buyers so not being to convince all of them is not entirely a loss. Because perhaps, you may be able to persuade 20 of these followers or friends to buy the product that you are selling, so that after all, the three minutes of clicking and tapping of updates just brought you 20 customers and that is not exactly that bad. The little effort you have put into social media marketing could translate to a huge and successful result.

Social media is definitely a cheap outlet to advertise, promote, and market your business. With a stable and reliable internet connection and gadget to use, you may already be ready to go build a base for your business. You just need to give in some little effort and you can already expect a great result. It is like putting in a cent and getting back a hundred bucks. So, of course, as a business, it is very important for you to take advantage of the advancements of technology and telecommunication by stepping up your business into the cyber world.

2 - Using Facebook in Social Media Marketing

Facebook is one of the most commonly used social networking website. There is a higher chance that a person has a Facebook account than not having one. A person may have a Facebook account in the same way that he or she has his or her own mobile number — it is more of a given. It is a platform that allows you to connect with people — schoolmates, classmates, acquaintances, ex-schoolmates, ex-classmates, workmates, relatives, and even ex-lovers. Facebook is website that connects people together despite the distance and time differences. But aside from connecting and reconnecting with friends, Facebook can also be used as a tool to sell and advertise.

Facebook has also designed itself to be business-friendly to those who want to earn money through the site whether they are a big-time or small enterprise.

Why Use Facebook for Social Media Marketing?

1. Encompassing

With everyone almost having a Facebook account, you can expect a lot of audience and possible customers. So that when you put up your business page, you are assured that a lot of people will be able to know about it.

2. Effective and Efficient

With just a few clicks and taps on your smartphone or your laptop, you will be able to reach a million audience whose attention you could possibly attract to the business that you have put up in the site.

3. Wide Array of Medium

Facebook allows you to use different types of medium to use. You can use photos, videos, or links to other websites as well.

4. Business-Friendly Functions

Facebook's pages include a measuring application that could tell how well your business is growing in terms of its activity in the social media site. Indicators such as the number of likes of the page, number of likes of your posts, number of views of the page, and even the reviews of the people of your product will give you an idea of how you are standing in the business field.

5. Customer-Friendly Functions

Your customers, whom you really are catering for, will be able to like your posts, rate and review your page and business and they also give feedback on your products and services through public comments. Their free and good testimonies will attract more customers or so you would know which parts of your business you should improve on.

How to use Facebook for Social Media Marketing

It is up to you if you want to create a public account, wherein people can add as a friend, or you can make your business page more impersonalized by setting up a page. For business reasons, a page is more highly recommended. But how do you start setting up one?

Step 1

If you already have a personal account, then you are now ready to set up your business page. Start by clicking the arrow icon on the top right corner of your homepage and select the tab that says "Create a Page".

Step 2

Fill up the contents needed for the page — from a little description of your business, your contact number, and if you have any store, you may also include your location or any landmark near to it and as well as your store hours.

Step 3

You may invite your friends in your personal account to like your page so they can get updates of your business or you can also share the page on your personal profile so your friends could visit it.

Step 4

After having your business page's likes, you can now calmly say to yourself that you have your market already. You may expand this from time to time by sharing your page every once in a while. But this time, entice your followers and likers by posting updates about your business. These updates could be of different mediums — you can use graphic posters, videos, or even simple statuses. Your posts could be a way to keep your customers close at hand because they get to know what is going on in your business. If you have promos or sales then you will be assured that even a simple announcement in your Facebook page can already inform a lot of people.

Being the administrator of the page, Facebook sends you weekly stats or you can check how your page is doing in terms of likes and views.

Facebook is an incredibly HUGE opportunity for your business, but also for individuals.

77% of businesses have acquired new customers through Facebook marketing alone (Marketing Charts).

3 - Using Instagram in Social Media Marketing

Visual content is getting popular in the social media most likely because they can immediately attract people. Instagram is one of the most common social media application that is mainly used in smartphones or iPhones. Although it can be accessed as a website, a user will not be able to make an account and upload a picture or photo into it. But still, Instagram is a very good avenue to put up your business too.

Why Use Instagram for Social Media Marketing

1. Handy

Among all the social media applications, Instagram is the most handy and specific when it comes to its purpose. Only pictures and videos may be posted through smartphones or tabs. However, this does not make Instagram less of an avenue for a business because it has avid users that a few taps and clicks can *talk to*.

2. Can Tap Other Social Networking Sites

Instagram has a feature that allows your posts to be posted on other social networking sites as well. So you do not only get to attract Instagram users but also users from the other sites in which your account is connected to. This way, your potential customers is not only limited.

3. Business Person-Friendly Functions

Having hashtags on your posts makes your photos and videos easier to find by Instagram users even though they are not exactly following you. The activity in Instagram is also very high that even people could see what photos were liked by their followers so discovering Instagram accounts is also very easy and fast. These advantages are often overlooked by many business people. According to Forrester's latest study, they found out that Instagram is more engagement generating as compared to Facebook and Twitter. Moreover, in an American Express Survey, it showed that only 2% of small enterprises utilize Instagram as a Social Media Marketing outlet. So if you are a business person, you may have your business on Instagram as your competitive advantage.

4. Customer-Friendly Functions

Because hashtags make a business person's post easier to find, customers will find it less of a hassle to look for products of their desire. They can just search the tags and they can already find your post. Instagram also features a function of suggesting who to follow so Instagram users may also find your profile. Lastly, Instagram allows easy interactions as well. When the business person posts an update through a photo or video, customers who are following him or her may immediately see the update and give a comment or showing his or her preference by liking the post. This way, customers can instantaneously give their feedback about the business.

How to use Instagram for Social Media Marketing

Step 1

Download and install Instagram on your smartphone, iPhone, or tab. After doing so, sign up and choose a username that is relevant to your business to make it less confusing to the customers. Then, fill in the basic information.

Step 2

You may now start posting photos of your products, teasers, sneak peeks, behind the scene photos, day-to-day office life, special offers or services, promos, or sales. Make sure that your photos or videos are presentable. These are the only mode of showing off your business so you have to make the most of them. Keep in mind that the clearer, less filtered, and appealing they are, the more they can attract followers and customers. Take these postings as make or break deals of your business.

Step 3

Then, you may proceed by following accounts to gain chances of them following you back. When you have assured that your photos and videos are well made, you may keep calm because followers could come to you. However, as a business, do not rely on customers finding you. Find customers as well by continuously following accounts whom you can target as customers. Some of the business owners who run their businesses in Instagram and leave comments in other people's photos saying that they should check out their account. This is one tactic that you may also use.

Step 4

Lastly, post hashtags on your posts to make them easily seen by other users who are looking for them. Then, connect your posts to your other social media accounts for a broader audience and target market.

4 - Using YouTube for Social Media Marketing

Some businessmen and women oversee YouTube as a social media site. Yes, it primarily involves hosting of videos but YouTube also allows you to comment, like, have friends, and even subscribe to channels wherein interaction among users may hype up.

Why Use YouTube for Social Media Marketing

1. Visual Medium is a Plus

Human beings easily get attracted to visual objects. So, YouTube's edge of having videos of long lengths and high quality as forms of marketing is an edge that it has over other social media networking sites.

2. Encompassing

YouTube videos may be linked to other social networking sites as well. This means that your potential market is not only limited to those who are in YouTube but also in other sites as well. These may even include non-YouTube users.

3. Business Person-Friendly Functions

YouTube allows you to see how many views your video has, how many likes it got, and how many subscribers and friends you have. These will help you assess your stand in the site.

4. Customer-Friendly Functions

In YouTube, aside from interaction that can come between the two parties, customers can also be passive clickers who can just click on your video and watch. They do not have to read an entire post, nor do they have to keep an eye on every update all throughout the day. They can just sit back, relax, and watch your sell your products and services.

How to Use YouTube for Social Media Marketing

Step 1

Start off by signing up in YouTube and create your own channel. Choose a legit-sounding and official username that would let the people know in an instant that it is a channel for your business. Then, fill out the needed information with a little background of your business.

Step 2

You may record a video of you as if you are talking to your customers or you may also make animated ads of your business to introduce your products and services to your customers. You may edit the video well and then render it. Once your video is ready, you may upload it on your channel.

Step 3

To get to have your audience, you may start following channels in YouTube as well. You could also link your video to your other social media networking sites to let other people see and hear about your business. The important part is, get your video known. Once the people see your video, this may spark up comments from them. So, respond accordingly.

5 - Using Twitter for Social Media Marketing

Twitter is a site that values interaction among its users who have their identity as social media beings who are hungry for new ideas, information, services, and products. So, if you are a business person who disregards putting up a business in a cyber area like this then you are missing out on a lot of possible customers.

Why Use Twitter for Social Media Marketing

1. Encompassing

Twitter also has 288 Million active users that you can target as your customers. Twitter's Retweet Function can help you spread out your posts even to those people who are not following you as long as they are following those who have retweeted your tweets.

2. Effective and Efficient

Twitter can spread information faster than Facebook since you can immediately see all the tweets in your home page as soon as they are posted by those people you follow. So when you have an update about your business, your followers can immediately see it, most especially when they are online.

3. Wide Array of Medium

People may say that twitter is all about tweeting and ramblings on text but that is not true. Twitter also features different mediums that you can use to advertise. It allows you to post pictures, short clips, video links, and even connect it with other social media networking sites.

4. Business-Friendly Functions

Like Facebook, your number of followers is also an indicator of how many first-hand prospect customers you have for your business. More so, Twitter also has indicators that could tell you how far your post has been disseminated and how many people have liked your tweet. Retweet and Favorite functions of Twitter can give you an idea of the traffic or activity of your business.

Hashtag and trending topics, which are primarily the hot talk-of-the-Twitter-Users will help in creating traffic about certain ideas and topics or happenings. As a business person, you may also take advantage of these Twitter functions. If your product or service becomes the talk of the Twitter users, the more people would want to know about it.

5. Customer-Friendly Functions

Twitter's immediate response rates can assure your customers that they can give you an immediate feedback on what they think about your product or service. They may use the reply button or mention function to tell you their opinions. Your customers' feedbacks may tell you how well you stand in your business so you may immediately respond to problems if you have to or you can keep up and improve what your customers appreciate of your business.

How to Use Twitter for Social Media Marketing?

To use twitter, you may immediately sign up an account for your business without the need of having a personal account. The moment you create an account, you can immediately use that for your business. This is how to start:

Step 1

You can either go to twitter.com using your laptop or personal computer or you can use your smartphone to download and install the application on your phone. The point is, you have to start by signing up either way.

Step 2

Fill up the needed parts of the information about your business, perhaps a short biography of it and contact details as well. Then make sure that your account is on public so customers who will be viewing your profile will be able to know immediately what your business is about.

Step 3

There is no point in having a Twitter account for your business when you have no followers, and with that, your tweets about your products and services will seem like you are speaking to thin air. So gain yourself some followers by following people on Twitter whom you see as possible customers. By following them, there will be a chance of having them check your profile and if they are interested in your business, they may follow back. So, that way, you will already have a first-hand target market for your business. Twitter has a "Who to Follow" area on the side of its pages so you will have an idea on who to follow as well.

Step 4

After having an audience or possible customers, you may now start tweeting or announcing promos, sales, or tag-liners of your product or service. Use hashtags that relate to your tweet and get it trending on Twitter. Also, encourage hearing from your followers as well. You may ask them what they think about your product. That way, you become an approachable business person whom the customers will find comfort in giving out their feedbacks for further improvement. Most of all, make sure that you update your profile every time.

6 - Using Tumblr for Social Media Networking

Tumblr is a both a blog and a social media networking site wherein the users can post what they want in their blogs and followers may reply, reblog, or like these posts. It is pretty much overlooked as a business avenue by many since it is majorly a blog but actually, Tumblr has features that may be used for social media marketing.

Why Use Tumblr for Social Media Marketing

1. Customizable

Among all the other social networking sites, Tumblr is the closest website that could help you in creating your business' own official website that is interactive to the customers. More than any other social media site, it is Tumblr that can give you the freedom to create a page that you can customize all you want. This is because it is a blog-social media site. The blog page that others may view can be edited and designed to your liking so that it would most likely reflect what your business is really like and what it is really for. You can make up your own color combinations, make your own themes, decide on the categorization of posts, and many more.

2. Posts Can Get Viral On Different Social Media Sites

A lot of posts — articles, photos, and videos — in other social networking sites started off in Tumblr. Tumblr posts could get viral and be linked to other sites as well. So you know that what you post in your blog could still get viral in other websites.

3. Local Going Global

Even if you are a small business, you may have dreams of shipping your products to other places to let your little business grow. Tumblr is then best for you. This is where you can find diverse people from different cultures and countries in just a single and easy group.

4. Business Person- Friendly Functions

Tumblr has Reblog and Tag functions that can help you in getting your posts around the website. The more Reblogs your post has, the more you know that a lot of blog users have seen it on their dashboards. And the Tags allow your post to be searched in the website so despite being non-followers of your blog, people may still be able to get to hear from your business. Tumblr also has the Likes function that allows you to know how many people have liked your post. You may also know the number of views that your page gets by putting up a counter on your blog. Some counters will tell you how many visits you had from different countries so you get to know who your usual audience are.

Moreover, Tumblr also allows you to use different types of medium for your posts. You may have videos, still pictures, animated pictures, photosets, links, quotes, and even music. So, as a business person in the website, you may utilize these functions to attract your followers to buy your product or service.

5. *Customer-Friendly Functions*

Even though Tumblr is known to be a blog site wherein the owners of the blogs can post what they want to, it still is open for social interaction among users and even non-users. An Ask Box is available on every account and it may be used by interested customers to tell the owner of the business blog what they think or what they want to know about the product. And as a business person, you may choose to answer the question privately or publicly, so that those who are concerned with the same question may also know the answer.

6. Tumblr also features a Reply function wherein followers of the blog may reply to the posts freely. This way, customers may be able to address their inquiries and comments immediately to your knowing.

How to Use Tumblr for Social Media Marketing

Step 1

You have to begin by making your own account and blog. But to your advantage, if you are a business person with a number of small businesses then you can just add a blog on the same primary account that you have made. Go to tumblr.com or install the application on your smartphone and get started with signing up.

Step 2

Before you add up the basic information about your business, you have to think of a domain name for your blog. This name has to be legit and formal so people would know that your business is a real one and not some spamming dealers. Choose your domain name wisely because it would reflect your business' image. After that, provide basic information regarding your business.

Step 3

The most challenging part in Tumblr is gaining followers. Some users have had their blogs for years and still have less than a hundred followers but if you are an active blogger who invests on promoting your blog then it is highly possible that you can earn a thousand followers in just a month or two.

You can start off by following bloggers whom you consider to be client prospects. Once they see that you have followed them, they may consider checking your blog out and once they see that you have presented well your posts and information, chances are they will follow you back. Then you get your first-hand possible customers. You may also tap on famous Tumblr users to include you in their promos so their followers would get to hear about your business. If this interests them then most likely, they would also follow your blog. Most of all, do not forget about using the hashtags. Some Tumblr users out there may want to follow your blog but they just have not heard about it yet. So by putting relevant tags on your posts, they will be able to find them just by searching them out in Tumblr.

Step 4

Now that you have followers, your posts and updates about your business will now have their audience. Use the different media and features of Tumblr to your advantage when you announce new items, promos, sales, and other events of your business and update every once in a while.

7 - Advanced Social Media Marketing Tips

The social media networking sites have their own identities as new outlets for advertising and marketing your products and even different platforms have different features that could help you. These outlets differ a lot from other avenues for selling your items and services, primarily as being the cheapest, most effective, most efficient, and easiest of all kinds of marketing avenues. However, social media marketing will not exactly result in success if the process of putting up the business in the cyber world's interactive sites is not well done. Some tips to make your social media marketing tactic successful are:

1. Utilize Different Functions and Features

Most platforms have common features like being able to have the contents shared to the public, getting feedbacks through comments or messaging, seeing likes or favorites of posts, and many more. But these social media networking sites also have features or characters that are unique in them that you can use to your advantage as a business person. Facebook is most commonly used, Twitter can update followers faster, Tumblr is customizable, Instagram is the simplest and handiest, and Google Plus is connected to an email. Now, it is up to you to use their defining edges to your advantage.

2. Make Profiles and Pages Appealing

Social networking sites are *social* because they generate interaction among the users. These users define how much activity is happening to your business and they all begin by getting to know its existence in the interactive sites. Keep in mind that the more appealing and beautified your posts are, the more people will become interested.

3. Do Not Forget Honesty

You may have beautified your photos, videos, or music to the maximum level that they do not entirely show the real product already. This is a big No-no in social media marketing. You are in the social media networking site to get closer to your customers easily so you could develop a strong customer-seller bond. And that is definitely not bound to happen if deception rules over your business.

4. Be Social to Customers

All these social media networking sites offer feedback functions from customers, as well as the account's administrator's functions to reply. Take these functions to their purpose and interact with your customers. Encourage them to give you their opinions of your products or services and when they do, respond as possible as you can and be polite. You can also thank customers who have patronized your products ever since or you can address those who have issues over your items as well. In any way that you can, make your social media marketing strategy really social.

5. Be Careful With What You Post

Internet posts can get really viral and this can either make or break your business. If the talk about your business is positive then good for you but if it's not, then you have to do some crisis management immediately. In order to avoid that, always be careful with what you post. Keep in mind that people of different races, ages, and genders are following your pages so avoid making advertisements or marketing strategies that may insult or come off as insensitive to people.

6. Take Note of the Indicators

All of these sites have features that could tell you how well you are doing as a social media business site. So, use these functions to continuously improve your business. Despite having a thousand likes or followers already, do not stop searching for more since there could be a lot more users out there who could be interested in what you can offer.

7. Update, update, and update

Your social media accounts will not buzz when they do not even contain anything that is of date. Let us put it this way, perhaps you have posted a photo of the menu of your little food business but that was 5 years ago and now the prices have changed already. So when a customer searches for your products your un-updated menu is what he or she will find. When that customer orders from you and find out that your prices have gone higher, do you think he or she will be happy? No. So make sure that what you have in your pages reflect your business' current state. This goes out to all other content of your page. So update, update, and update.

8 – How You Can Build An Effective Social Media Marketing Strategy

"Companies should focus more on how to BE social, and less on how to DO social media."

Step #1: Set your goal and stick to it

The first step to any social media marketing strategy is to establish clear objectives and goals that you hope to achieve.

You simply can't move forward in your business if you don't know what you're working toward. You need to have a clear, huge vision.

Look closely at your company's overall needs and decide how you want to use social media to contribute to reaching them.

Having these objectives in your mind also allows you to quickly react when social media campaigns are not meeting your expectations: it can happen. Strive to approach these goals using the S.M.A.R.T. approach: this means that they should all be specific, measurable, attainable, relevant and time-bound.

Keep in mind that if you have no execution strategy, your content is likely going to fall through the cracks.

For example, let's say you decide to use Twitter in order to promote your brand.

First of all, set a limit on how many tweets you have to publish per day. This number can be adjusted as needed, but having a number you have to hit, even something as small as four tweets per day, gives you a benchmark and a goal at the very least.

Look at your competitors and try to investigate how often they are posting and conduct industry research to see the ideal amount of content to publish per day on each channel. You want to be active, but not overly active.

Compile all the content in an easy-to-read editorial calendar. Google Excel Docs is a good place to start. Set up a weekly, shareable publishing calendar, then separate by social channel, and provide columns for co-workers within your team to provide their feedback before posting. Plan your calendar ahead, but continue making additions if necessary.

Look into **social media management platforms**, like TweetDeck, Buffer, and Hootsuite, to help you schedule posts ahead of time, monitor and manage your social feeds, and access performance analytics.

Step #2: Treat each channel as an individual entity

Each social channel needs to be treated as a separate entity, because they're different from each other. There can be content that is spread across all channels: for example, if your business was recently acquired by a global company, this is likely news you want to share across the board. But, generally, you should adjust your content strategy depending on the audience for that channel.

For example, LinkedIn tends to have a more business-focused audience looking for in-depth, educational content, compared to Instagram, which is likely to have an audience looking for engaging visual content, pictures and videos. Pay attention to your followers demographic on each channel to publish content that appeals to them.

...which leads us to Step #3...

Step #3: Identify your Ideal Customers

Buyer personas help you define and target the right people, in the right places, at the right times with the right messages.

When you know your target audience's age, interests, occupation, income, habits, pains, problems, obstacles, likes, dislikes, objections and motivations, then it's easier and cheaper to target them on socials or any other media.

Being specific is paramount to your success: the more specific you are, the more conversions you're going to get out of every channel you use to promote your business.

There is a business rule that says that it costs 4 to 10 times more to acquire a customer than to retain one. In order to keep your customers around, use social media as a tool to support, communicate and engage them. A good social relationship with your customers should translate into a better perception and offline relationship with your brand. By developing a strong social bond, customers will be more likely to stick with your brand and your products time and time again.

Whether someone is commenting on a post of yours, writing on your wall or mentioning you on Twitter, it's important to always communicate and stay engaged. A recent social study showed that 5 in 6 messages on social requiring response are not answered by brands. If customers are consistently ignored, they'll probably ditch your brand all together and eventually look for an alternative.

Make sure to respond to customers who have left negative feedback about your brand as well. Too many companies have lost favor with their fans because they deleted negative reviews or messages, trying to hide them.

Due to the lack of communication, the dissatisfied potential lead is now turning to your competitors to seek answers to their questions. On the other hand, when you're able to deliver a thoughtful response in a timely manner that visitor is flattered and intrigued by your brand. It's humanizing to take the time to respond to a personal inquiry, and it builds your authority in that market.

Always respond with patience and respect to negative feedbacks: think of your social channels as an opportunity to display how awesome you treat your customers.

Step #4: Create a Content Strategy

It's time to develop your messages!

Now that you have a handle on your ideal customers and your competition, it's finally time to start building your messages. This isn't detailed content; rather it's the key messages that you think will resonate with your customers, based on the personas you have created before. Choose two or three messages, then break each one down another level creating a simple and clear messaging hierarchy.

There's nothing wrong with adopting some of your competitors' successful messaging ideas but also try to create original messages that set you apart. This will help you to create your unique brand voice. Don't be afraid to get creative as your social media presence should not be boring, but exciting!

As I told you before, when it comes to social media, your competition can tell you a lot about what works and what doesn't. After all, they're targeting the same customers you are.

If you ignore your competition, you're giving up a fantastic opportunity to learn from their successes and mistakes and save a lot of time and money.

To research your competitors, start by picking three or four of the top ones. Find out which social networks they're active on, and study their content. Do they talk about their products, or do they focus on other things? Is it funny or serious? What kind of cultural references do they use?

Then, take a look at how well each competitor is doing (e.g. how much engagement, comments, shares, likes they get on their updates.) This will let you determine which strategies work and which ones don't.

Content and social media have a symbiotic relationship: without great content social media is meaningless and without social media nobody will know about your content. Use them together to reach and convert your prospects.

There are three main components to any successful social media content strategy: the **type** of content, the **time** of posting and the **frequency** of posting.

The type of content you should post on each social network relies on form and context. Form is how you present that information—text only, images, links, video, etc.

Context fits with your company voice and platform trends. Should your content be funny, serious, highly detailed and educational or something else?

There are many studies that give you a specific time when you should post on social media.

Facebook: the research shows that 86% of posts are published during the work week with engagement peaking on Thursday and Friday. Of course, the less people want to be at work, the more they are on Facebook.

The best time of the day to post is early afternoon. At 3pm you'll get the most clicks, but anytime between 9am to 7pm is good.

Twitter: engagement for brands is 175 higher on weekends. The best time to tweet is 5pm if you want to be retweeted, or 12pm and 6pm for the highest CTR (Click-Through Rate) – probably because of lunch breaks and people looking for something to keep them occupied.

LinkedIn: the best days to post are Tuesdays, Wednesdays and Thursdays. According to LinkedIn itself, weekdays during business hours are the best time to post.

Instagram: the engagement stays consistent throughout the week, with slight spikes on

Mondays and a slight dip on Sundays. The best time to post is the off work hours.

Google+: the best days to post are the weekdays. Posts on Wednesdays at 9am do the best in terms of social applause and engagement.

However, I suggest using those studies as guidelines rather than hard rules. Remember, your audience is unique, so you need to test and figure out the best time for yourself.

Posting frequency is as important as the content you share. You don't want to annoy your fans or followers posting too much.

Finding the perfect frequency is crucial because it could mean more engagement for your content or more dislikes and unfollows. For example, you could use Facebook Insights or Fanpage Karma to see when your fans are online and engaging with your content on Facebook; use the tool Followerwonk for Twitter; use Timing+ for Google+.

Step #5: Test, evaluate and adjust your social media marketing plan

To find out which adjustments need to be made to your social media marketing strategy, you should constantly be testing new ways and plans. Build testing capabilities into every action you take on social networks. Track your links using URL shorteners (such as bitly.com). Use Hootsuite's social media analytics to track the success and reach of social campaigns. Track page visits driven by social media with Google analytics. Always record and analyze your successes and failures, and then adjust your social media marketing plans in response.

Surveys are also a great way you can gauge success. Ask your social media followers, email lists and website visitors how you're doing on social media. This direct approach is often very effective. Then ask your offline customers if social media had a role in their purchasing. This insight will be huge when you look for where to improve.

The most important thing to understand about your social media plan is that it should be constantly changing. As new networks emerge, you may want to add them to your plan. As you achieve your goals, you need to adjust them or find new goals for each network. New challenges might present themselves. As you scale your business, you might need to add new roles or grow your social presence for different branches or countries.

Be flexible and open-minded.

Conclusion

Thank you again for reading this book!

This short, practical guide gave you all the basic information you need in order to start marketing your business on social medias. I hope it was able to help you understand fully the importance of social media marketing and the degree of advantage it gives you for you to grow your business.

In this modern age where everything spreads like the speed of a bullet, you need to plan out and carefully consider strategies for you so you won't be left out.

Connect with potential and current customers and make your brand stand out in your market!

The next step is to engage in updating your social media networking sites religiously to keep a steady bond with your market.

That's really the FUTURE of marketing. TAKE ACTION TODAY!

Thank you and good luck!

Jason Roberts

www.ingramcontent.com/pod-product-compliance
Lightning Source LLC
Chambersburg PA
CBHW070842220526
45466CB00002B/850